Other titles in the series:
The Crazy World of Aerobics (Bill Stott)
The Crazy World of Cats (Bill Stott)
The Crazy World of Cricket (Bill Stott)
The Crazy World of Gardening (Bill Stott)
The Crazy World of Golf (Mike Scott)
The Crazy World of the Greens (Barry Knowles)
The Crazy World of the Handyman (Roland Fiddy)
The Crazy World of Hospitals (Bill Stott)
The Crazy World of Learning to Drive (Bill Stott)
The Crazy World of Love (Roland Fiddy)
The Crazy World of Marriage (Bill Stott)
The Crazy World of the Office (Bill Stott)
The Crazy World of Photography (Bill Stott)
The Crazy World of Rugby (Bill Stott)
The Crazy World of Sailing (Peter Rigby)
The Crazy World of Sex (David Pye)

This paperback edition published simultaneously in 1992 by Exley
Publications Ltd. in Great Britain, and Exley Giftbooks in the USA.
First hardback edition published in Great Britain in 1989 by Exley
Publications Ltd.

Reprinted 1992 and 1993 (twice)

ISBN 1-85015-314-0

Printed in Spain by Grafo S.A., Bilbao.

Exley Publications Ltd, 16 Chalk Hill, Watford, Herts WD1 4BN,
United Kingdom.
Exley Giftbooks, 359 East Main Street, Suite 3D, Mount Kisco,
NY 10549, USA.

the CRAZY world of HOUSEWORK

Cartoons by Bill Stott

EXLEY

MT. KISCO, NEW YORK • WATFORD, UK

"I'm sorry to drag you out, Doctor – I'm worried sick about him – he keeps tidying his room up."

"Mom! Dad got the numbers on the washing machine wrong again."

"And when Cinderella had all the housework to do, did she say 'bloody' all the time like you?"

"I don't know. I was dusting. I got bored."

"O.K. Killer – what shall we do first – junior's bedroom? The hall? The living room?"

"Have you seen my running shoes?"

"O.K. – the house is pristine. You have exactly 12 hours
to wreck it."

"*Dad? I think I just did a bad thing.*"

"Don't ask. My wife and I swapped jobs. She went to the office and I ran the house. She was so good they have made her manager and fired me."

"All I did was ask her if she'd like a new vacuum cleaner for her birthday ..."

"Somebody's going to have to own up about leaving the shower dirty – it's getting cold ..."

"Hello Darling, I'm home. Good day?"

"Now, little man – has the nasty lady been cruel to you?"

"Definite smear, bottom left-hand corner ..."

"This – iron. You-iron-shirts. I-go-out-with-the-girls. O.K.?"

"Looks like you have an interesting evening
ahead of you, Clive ..."

"'Course – I've told your mother many times – with a little organization – housework would take about thirty minutes a day ..."

"What a great shot! Quick, or you'll miss the replay!"

"'Course – we saved a lot. Gerry fitted it – all by himself. Didn't you Gerry?"

"If cleaning the stove is <u>my</u> job – I do it <u>my</u> way – O.K.?"

"He's right. There _is_ something living under the microwave ... "

"The lady on the T.V. smiles and laughs when she uses 'Glimshine' Mommy. Why aren't you smiling and laughing?"

"Mom! Mom! Sandy's thrown up in my toy box!"

"It __always__ sucks the dog up on full power – don't you know anything?"

"*Do your parents do this? The only time I have to tidy up is when the cleaning lady is coming!*"

"Quick – more ketchup. They'll never guess how we did this!"

"And be sure to stack the dishwasher properly ..."

"And here on the home straight managing director, alias Mrs. Brownlow, needs a new lap record if she's going to make work on time …"

"Oh no, it's weird Mr. Weitz – you know, the 'new man' who actually _discusses_ soap powder!"

"Quick – put that back and move to the expensive wine – here come the Smiths!"

"*Your father's doing the washing today – just as soon as he's figured out how to open the carton ...*"

*"There's my little treasure – busy polishing the table
with fly spray."*

"And while in the shower, you had a life and death struggle with an enraged bull elephant did you?"

"So, the dog wrecked the kitchen floor? In his own shoes, or yours?"

"A feather duster? You dust feathers? I didn't know we had any!"

"You got the cat 'Prettypaws'. She hates 'Prettypaws'."

"Mother says: 'Have you dusted this week?'."

"Hello Grandma! We knew you were coming because
Daddy tidied up."

"Will we share everything, when we're married? – Sure – housework – kids – everything – trust me ..."

"Fair exchange? He decides what our stance is on nuclear disarmament, the Middle East and inflation and I do the cooking, decorating and shopping."

"Today – I thought – I'll be positive. Today I will organize myself. Today I will turn washing and ironing into an art form. Then I thought 'Stuff it' and had a glass of sherry."

"I just can't decide whether to use the deep family system, the all-in economy cycle or the standard wash ..."

"*Correct me if I'm mistaken Farthingale, but the thumb print on her ladyship's white wine glass is not one of ours.*"

"*I wonder if we could all stand and move our chairs a little?*
They make such horrid marks on the carpet."

"Dad! She's talking to the ironing again ..."

"Me, obsessed with housework? Don't be silly!"

"The tumbler dryer's bust, the vacuum's bunged up, my three-year-old's got chickenpox – and you want to know how I feel about double glazing? Clear off!"

WOW! THE DISHWASHER BROKE, I GOT A PARKING TICKET OUTSIDE SCHOOL . . . WHAT ELSE CAN GO WRONG?

"The shelf's up, Darling!"

"O.K. Let's just run through it again – 'Turbobrite' for the bathroom, 'Wonderwood' for the furniture, 'Luvvarug' for the carpets ..."

"I tidied my room. Can I go out now?"

"Look Dad, we're helping. We emptied the vacuum."

"Come quick – we toilet-trained the dog!"

"Keep it straight, Son, keep it straight ..."

"I was a little tetchy at teatime after the tumble dryer blew up just as the kids knocked over the tropical fish tank. Sigmund Freud here wondered if I'd got PMS."

"Guess what! Today I washed the 5,798th sock
since we were married!"

"And while you were at the shops, the cat got in the tumble dryer ..."

"It's all right – poor soul's just realized you're off school for the next six weeks ..."

"My God! What happened? It looks like you had a baby elephant through here!"

"The money and valuables I found in the filter are worth more than the machine!"

"Your mother's feeling better? That's good.
Yes, everything's fine here ..."

"Come and look! – Baby Sheridan's on the television ..."

"Dad! Mom murdered the vacuum cleaner!"

"My status? You can put me down as a presently inactive science graduate who's spent the last seven years raising kids, shopping, ironing, dusting and cooking."

"Would you like me to move?"

"We made you a cup of tea!"

"You don't mind tea in the hall do you? The lounge carpet is new."

"You know there's probably dust on top of the display cabinet. I know there's probably dust on top of the display cabinet, but the Simpsons, who are due here for dinner in five minutes, probably don't."

"*This is a recorded message. As you may have noticed, I am not here. Dinner will be indefinitely postponed. I have run away. There is a casserole in the cooker. The bills have been paid. Goodbye.*"

"*Of course you hate housework. I couldn't possibly love a woman who <u>liked</u> housework.*"

"Gary won't be arriving tonight. We're into role reversal – so tell me a filthy joke."

"Looks like furniture polish poisoning ..."

"Hmm – 'Imparts a brilliant shine on all domestic surfaces' …"

Books in the "Crazy World" series
($4.99 £2.99 paperback)

The Crazy World of Aerobics (Bill Stott)
The Crazy World of Cats (Bill Stott)
The Crazy World of Cricket (Bill Stott)
The Crazy World of Gardening (Bill Stott)
The Crazy World of Golf (Mike Scott)
The Crazy World of the Greens (Barry Knowles)
The Crazy World of The Handyman (Roland Fiddy)
The Crazy World of Hospitals (Bill Stott)
The Crazy World of Housework (Bill Stott)
The Crazy World of Learning (Bill Stott)
The Crazy World of Love (Roland Fiddy)
The Crazy World of Marriage (Bill Stott)
The Crazy World of The Office (Bill Stott)
The Crazy World of Photography (Bill Stott)
The Crazy World of Rugby (Bill Stott)
The Crazy World of Sailing (Peter Rigby)
The Crazy World of Sex (David Pye)

Books in the "Mini Joke Book" series
($6.99 £3.99 hardback)

These attractive 64 page mini joke books are illustrated throughout by Bill Stott.

A Binge of Diet Jokes
A Bouquet of Wedding Jokes
A Feast of After Dinner Jokes
A Knockout of Sports Jokes
A Portfolio of Business Jokes
A Round of Golf Jokes
A Romp of Naughty Jokes
A Spread of Over-40s Jokes
A Tankful of Motoring Jokes

Books in the "Fanatics" series
($4.99 £2.99 paperback)

The **Fanatic's Guides** are perfect presents for everyone with a hobby that has got out of hand. Eighty pages of hilarious black and white cartoons by Roland Fiddy.

The Fanatic's Guide to the Bed
The Fanatic's Guide to Cats
The Fanatic's Guide to Computers
The Fanatic's Guide to Dads
The Fanatic's Guide to Diets
The Fanatic's Guide to Dogs
The Fanatic's Guide to Husbands
The Fanatic's Guide to Money
The Fanatic's Guide to Sex
The Fanatic's Guide to Skiing

Books in the "Victim's Guide" series
($4.99 £2.99 paperback)

Award winning cartoonist Roland Fiddy sees the funny side to life's phobias, nightmares and catastrophes.

The Victim's Guide to the Dentist
The Victim's Guide to the Doctor
The Victim's Guide to Middle Age

Great Britain: Order these super books from your local bookseller or from Exley Publications Ltd, 16 Chalk Hill, Watford, Herts WD1 4BN. (Please send £1.30 to cover postage and packing on 1 book, £2.60 on 2 or more books.)